Burning Cash in the Warehouse

Identify 7 Costly Errors & Build 3 step Profit Engine

Rohit Patravali

FanatiXx Publication

FanatiXx® Publication

Mumbai | Ahmedabad | Delhi NCR | Rourkela
ISO 9001:2015 Certified

By: Rohit Patravali

ISBN: 978-93-7406-228-9

Book: Burning Cash in the Warehouse
Price: INR 199/-

Printing By: BooksClub.in

To my mother Mrs. Rohini Patravali, who has moved Heaven and Earth to see me alive when I was born.

My only source of Strength.

Acknowledgement

First and foremost, I would like to express my deepest gratitude to my mother, wife and my children. Your unwavering support, patience, and understanding have been the foundation of my work and the true inspiration behind this book. Thank you for giving me the time and space to pursue this passion.

My sincerest thanks go to the mentors, teachers and industry veterans whose wisdom and insights have shaped my understanding of logistics. Your guidance has been invaluable.

To my colleagues and team members, thank you for your hard work and for inspiring me daily with your dedication and innovation. This book would not have been possible without your contributions and the real-world challenges we have navigated together.

This book is the culmination of years of experience and is a testament to the support and collaboration of many individuals. I would like to express my deepest gratitude to all those who played a role in bringing this work to life.

Finally, to my family and friends, thank you for your patience, support, and encouragement throughout this journey. Your understanding has been the foundation of my work.

I hope this book serves its purpose, empowering business owners and professionals to master the art of logistics and turn their operations into a source of growth.

Table of Contents

Chapter 1: 3

Location, Location, Lost Profits: The Hidden Costs of a Poorly Chosen Warehouse 3

Chapter 2: 7

The Bottleneck at Your Bays 7

Chapter 3: 11

Foundation Failures: Compromising on Plinth and Clear Height Costs You Dearly 11

Chapter 4: 16

The Floor is the Foundation of Efficiency (and Profit): Why Quality Matters 16

Chapter 5: 20

Suffocating Profits: The Hidden Costs of Poor Ventilation 20

Chapter 6: 24

Settling for Less: The False Economy of a Storage Shed 24

Chapter 7: 27

Overlooking the Human Element and Essential Infrastructure: Hidden Costs in Labor and Logistics 27

Chapter 8: 31

Optimizing Your Warehouse Layout: The Foundation of Efficient Operations 31

Chapter 9: 36

Investing in the Right Physical Storage and Handling Infrastructure: The Engine of Operational Efficiency 36

Chapter 10: 46

The Hidden Costs of Person-Based Operations............................ 46

Chapter 11: 50

From Individual Effort to Systemic Efficiency: A Roadmap to Process-Based Operations 50

Chapter 12: 58

Retaining Top Talent: Building a Culture of Value and Growth.... 58

Chapter 13: 64

The Perils of Poor Inventory Management: A Recipe for Financial Disaster.. 64

Chapter 14: 71

Leveraging Technology for Warehouse Efficiency 71

Chapter 15: 81

Transportation: Mastering the Flow of Goods.............................. 81

Chapter 16: 91

Shielding Your Assets: Essential Insurance for Warehouse Risks . 91

A

Infrastructure

For more than 20 years, I've lived the warehouse life, moving my business from one rented space to another. Each time, the story was the same: our primary concern was the rent. Everything else, from the ceiling height to the quality of the flooring and the loading bays, was a secondary consideration, often compromised to fit our budget.

This approach, driven by a desire for low costs, ended up being a costly mistake. We'd outgrow a space, and the nightmare of moving would begin. The expense of relocating all our goods, infrastructure, and office setups was a heavy blow to our bottom line, a financial hit we felt for years. We were always playing catch-up, making do with spaces that didn't truly serve our needs.

I've learned this lesson the hard way, and now I can spot these same mistakes when I visit other businesses. I see the invisible costs of poor infrastructure, the wasted time, the damaged goods, the inefficient operations, all slowly eroding a company's profits. Business owners, unknowingly, are letting their warehouses become a financial drain.

This experience has taught me a crucial lesson: The true cost of a warehouse isn't just the rent you pay each month. It's the silent killer of your profitability, the hidden expenses that accumulate from a poorly chosen space. By focusing on rent alone, you're not saving money; you're setting yourself up for a future of unnecessary expenses and operational headaches.

Chapter 1:

Location, Location, Lost Profits: The Hidden Costs of a Poorly Chosen Warehouse

The well-known real estate mantra, "location, location, location," is equally, if not more, critical for warehouses. While a warehouse's location seems like a one-time decision, a poor choice can silently erode your profits through a ripple effect of hidden costs.

Consider your warehouse's position relative to your suppliers, customers, and key transportation routes. A seemingly small locational disadvantage can lead to significant financial burdens over time.

- Increased Transportation Expenses: A warehouse situated far from suppliers or customers leads to higher inbound and outbound freight costs, cutting directly into your profit margins.
- Time and Delays: An inconvenient location results in longer lead times for receiving and shipping, which can damage your reputation and lead to lost sales.
- The Human Factor: A poor location with difficult commutes or a lack of public transport can make it hard to attract and retain staff, leading to higher recruitment and training costs.

- Logistical Nightmares: Placing a warehouse in a "no-entry zone" for trucks during the day forces operations into the night, increasing freight costs and causing frustration for drivers.
- Constrained Future Growth: A poorly located warehouse may lack space for expansion, forcing a costly relocation down the line when the business needs to grow.

Potential Financial Losses

The combined impact of a sub-optimal warehouse location can lead to a significant financial drain, potentially ranging from 2% to 8% of your total sales revenue.

Ask Yourself:

- What is the annual spend on inbound and outbound transportation due to your location?
- What is the financial cost of delays and lost sales caused by your location?
- What is the cost of employee turnover related to the warehouse's location?
- What are the added costs of working around restricted logistics hours?
- Does your warehouse have room to expand, or will relocation be necessary for future growth?

Conclusion

A poorly located warehouse is a hidden drain on profits, inflating transportation costs, creating logistical bottlenecks, and challenging talent retention. Recognizing these expenses is the first step toward transforming this liability into a foundational asset for your profit engine.

Chapter 2:
The Bottleneck at Your Bays

Burning Cash in the Warehouse

Imagine your loading docks as the crucial entry and exit points of your warehouse. When there are too few or they are poorly designed, your operation can suffer from a bottleneck, leading to inefficiencies, delays, and a drain on profitability. A common and costly error is overlooking the impact of limited loading and unloading bays on your entire workflow.

When trucks are consistently waiting for an available bay, it actively erodes your bottom line in several ways:

- Skyrocketing Demurrage and Detention Charges: This is the most immediate financial hit. Every minute a truck waits to be unloaded costs you in demurrage and detention fees, which accumulate rapidly.
- Driver Dissatisfaction and Reduced Carrier Willingness: Long wait times frustrate truck drivers, making your warehouse an undesirable destination. This can lead to carriers becoming less willing to work with you or charging higher rates.

- Higher Freight Costs: When carriers experience consistent delays at your docks, they build this inefficiency into their pricing, leading to increased freight costs for you.
- Reduced Truck Utilization: From the carrier's perspective, their trucks are making less money per day when they are stuck in a queue, reducing their fleet's overall utilization.
- Increased Safety Hazards: Congested loading areas with limited space for trucks and forklifts significantly increase the risk of accidents, leading to costly repairs and potential injuries.

Optimizing Your Dock Operations

To avoid these costly issues, consider these aspects of your loading dock infrastructure:

- Number of Bays vs. Volume: Do you have enough bays to handle your peak traffic volume without creating queues?
- Strategic Dock Design: Is your dock layout designed for smooth truck flow, easy maneuvering, and quick access to staging areas?
- Clear Communication and Scheduling: Can you implement a scheduling system to reduce wait times and clearly communicate with drivers about procedures?

Potential Financial Losses

The total financial losses from limited loading and unloading docks can range from 1.25% to 6.7% of your total sales revenue, depending on the severity of the bottleneck.

Ask yourself:

- What are the demurrage or detention costs due to limited loading bays?
- What is the lost productivity cost from truck congestion?
- What is the financial impact of safety issues or lost customers from delays?

Conclusion

Your loading dock is a critical artery; inefficiencies here directly translate into costly demurrage fees, unproductive labor, sales loss, and frustrated carriers. By addressing these bottlenecks, you unlock significant savings and enhance overall operational rhythm, paving the way for a smoother, more profitable supply chain.

Chapter 3:

Foundation Failures: Compromising on Plinth and Clear Height Costs You Dearly

While external factors like location are crucial, a warehouse's internal structural elements, plinth height, and clear height are equally vital for efficiency, safety, and long-term usability. Overlooking these basic specifications can lead to a cascade of costly problems.

- Plinth: The raised base of the warehouse floor, lifting it above the surrounding ground.
- Clear Height: The usable vertical space from the floor to the lowest obstruction.

Compromising on either of these can severely restrict your operational capabilities and erode profits.

The Low Plinth Penalty: Inviting Trouble from the Ground Up

An inadequate plinth height (ideally around 4.5 feet) can expose your warehouse to significant risks and costs, especially in areas with heavy rain or varying ground conditions.

- Water Damage: A low plinth makes your warehouse vulnerable to flooding, which can damage inventory and lead to costly clean-ups and insurance claims.
- Pest Infestation: A ground-level floor provides easier access for pests, which can contaminate products and lead to financial losses. A raised plinth acts as a natural barrier.
- Loading and Unloading Headaches: A low plinth creates a height difference between the warehouse floor and truck beds, making loading and unloading difficult, time-consuming, and potentially dangerous.

The Ceiling Constraint: Bottlenecking Vertical Efficiency

While a clear height of 12-14 feet might seem sufficient, a modern distribution warehouse often needs closer to 20 feet. The difference has a profound impact on storage capacity and material handling.

- Wasted Vertical Space: A low clear height limits your ability to use vertical storage effectively, forcing you to use lower racking systems. This wasted space translates to higher storage costs per unit and may necessitate a larger, more expensive warehouse.
- Material Handling Limitations: A low ceiling restricts your choice of equipment, forcing you to use less space-efficient and more labour-intensive methods.

- Future Growth Obstacles: A low clear height will become a major constraint as your business grows, making it difficult to expand storage capacity within your existing facility.

Potential Financial Losses

- Low Plinth Height: The impact can range from 0.5% to 5.0% or higher of annual sales, depending on the frequency and severity of water damage and the value of goods stored.
- Low Clear Height: The losses can range from 0.5% to 3.0% of your total sales revenue, varying with the severity of the vertical bottleneck.

Ask yourself:

- Have low plinth heights led to water damage or pest access?
- Is the height difference between your floor and truck beds causing safety risks or delays?
- Is your current clear height limiting vertical storage, equipment options, or future growth?

Conclusion

The plinth and clear height are foundational elements that directly impact efficiency and long-term costs. Strategically addressing these aspects is crucial for building a resilient, cost-effective warehouse that supports your profit-generating activities.

Chapter 4:

The Floor is the Foundation of Efficiency (and Profit): Why Quality Matters

The warehouse floor is the foundation of your entire operation, supporting the constant traffic of forklifts and bearing the weight of your inventory. A high-quality floor is a strategic investment; a low-quality one is a hidden expense that can lead to a multitude of costly problems.

The Hidden Costs of Low-Quality Flooring

- Increased Equipment Wear: Uneven or damaged floors put excessive strain on forklifts and other equipment, leading to higher maintenance costs and shorter lifespans.
- Damage to Goods: Bumpy floors can cause vibrations and instability, increasing the risk of inventory being damaged during transport.
- Reduced Operational Speed: Equipment must move more slowly over poor flooring to avoid damage, leading to significant time inefficiencies and reduced throughput.
- Safety Hazards: Cracks, holes, and uneven surfaces create tripping hazards for staff and increase the risk of accidents involving forklifts.

- Dust Accumulation: Low-quality concrete can generate dust that contaminates inventory and creates a health hazard for employees, adding to cleaning costs.
- Higher Maintenance Costs: Poor flooring is harder to clean and maintain, and may require significant repair or replacement expenses over time.

The Benefits of High-Quality Flooring

Investing in a high-quality option like Vacuum Dewatered Flooring (VDF) is a smart move for a distribution warehouse.

- Exceptional Durability: VDF creates a dense, strong surface that can withstand heavy loads and constant traffic, leading to a longer lifespan and fewer repairs.
- Smooth and Level Surface: The smooth finish of VDF allows for faster and more efficient movement of equipment, reducing travel times and increasing throughput.
- Reduced Equipment Wear: A smooth surface minimizes stress on equipment, leading to lower maintenance costs.
- Minimized Dust: VDF significantly reduces dust generation, creating a cleaner and healthier environment.
- Enhanced Safety: A level and well-maintained VDF surface reduces tripping hazards and provides a stable platform for forklift operations.

- Lower Long-Term Costs: While the initial investment may be higher, the durability of VDF leads to significantly lower maintenance and repair costs over the long term.

Potential Financial Losses

The combined impact of low-quality warehouse flooring can range from 0.5% to 3.0% of your total annual sales revenue, and potentially higher for businesses with high-value goods.

Ask yourself:

- What are the annual costs for floor repair and maintenance?
- What is the annual cost of equipment repairs due to the floor's condition?
- What is the loss from inventory damage due to a substandard floor?

Conclusion

Your warehouse floor is a critical, yet often overlooked, element of your operation. A substandard floor accelerates equipment wear, compromises safety, and demands costly repairs. Prioritizing quality flooring protects your assets, empowers your workforce, and provides a stable foundation for profitability.

Chapter 5:

Suffocating Profits: The Hidden Costs of Poor Ventilation

In a busy warehouse, the quality of the air can have a significant, though often unseen, impact on profitability. Poor ventilation is more than just stuffy air; it can lead to a cascade of issues affecting your employees, your inventory, and your overall operational efficiency.

The Invisible Drain: How Poor Ventilation Eats Away at Your Profits

- Employee Health and Productivity: Poor air quality from dust, fumes, and inadequate fresh air circulation can lead to health issues, fatigue, and decreased concentration among staff. This results in lower productivity, increased absenteeism, and higher healthcare costs.
- Damage to Sensitive Goods: Poor ventilation can lead to damaging humidity and temperature fluctuations, causing condensation, mold growth, or spoilage of sensitive inventory.
- Regulatory Non-Compliance: Depending on your inventory and local regulations, inadequate ventilation can lead to non-compliance with health and safety standards, resulting in fines.

- Higher Energy Costs: In some cases, poor ventilation can lead to an overuse of air conditioning or heating to compensate, resulting in unnecessarily high energy bills.
- Reduced Employee Morale: Working in an uncomfortable and potentially unhealthy environment can lead to higher employee turnover, increasing recruitment and training costs.

The Importance of Proper Ventilation

Effective ventilation is crucial for:

- Good Air Quality: Introducing fresh air and removing pollutants like dust and fumes.
- Temperature and Humidity Control: Preventing fluctuations that can damage goods and create an uncomfortable environment.
- A Healthy and Safe Workplace: Contributing to the well-being and productivity of your employees.

Key Considerations for Effective Ventilation

- Natural Ventilation: Using strategically placed vents, louvers, and roof openings to allow for natural airflow. This is often the most cost-effective solution.
- Mechanical Ventilation: Employing fans, exhaust systems, and air handling units to actively circulate air. This is often necessary for larger warehouses.

- Combination Systems: Integrating both natural and mechanical ventilation for optimal airflow and energy efficiency.
- Specific Needs: Certain types of inventories, such as chemicals or perishable goods, require specialized ventilation.

Potential Financial Losses

The combined impact of poor warehouse ventilation can range from 0.5% to 4.0% of your total annual sales revenue, and potentially higher for businesses dealing with highly sensitive goods or operating in extreme climates.

Ask yourself:

- Is poor air quality affecting employee absenteeism?
- Do you experience losses from damage and spoilage of sensitive inventory?
- What are the cleaning costs for dust, mildew, and mold accumulation?

Conclusion

Poor warehouse ventilation leads to a cascade of hidden expenses: sick days, diminished output, damaged inventory, and increased cleaning. By rectifying these issues, you foster a healthier environment, prevent spoilage, and improve operational efficiency, breathing new life into your profit margins.

Chapter 6:

Settling for Less: The False Economy of a Storage Shed

In an effort to minimize initial costs, some business owners might use a storage shed instead of a purpose-built warehouse. This often proves to be a false economy, as the initial savings are quickly erased by a multitude of operational inefficiencies, limitations, and lost profits.

A storage shed is designed for simple storage, not for the dynamic environment of a distribution hub with constant receiving, storing, picking, and shipping. Trying to use a shed for these complex operations is inefficient and will inevitably lead to problems that can also affect a poorly designed warehouse.

The Long-Term Perspective

While a storage shed's initial cost may be appealing, its long-term inefficiencies, potential for inventory damage, safety risks, and limitations on growth will almost certainly outweigh any upfront savings. A properly designed warehouse provides a solid foundation for efficient operations, scalability, and sustained profitability.

Potential Financial Losses

The combined impact of using an inadequate shed instead of a warehouse can range from 2% to 10% or higher of your total annual sales revenue, especially for businesses with significant storage or distribution needs.

Ask yourself:

- What limitations are you facing with your current distribution facility?
- Will your current facility support your plans for future business growth?

Conclusion

While seemingly cost-saving, a "cheap" storage shed is a deceptive trap that leads to magnified long-term costs. A purpose-built warehouse offers the structural integrity and infrastructure needed for efficient, safe, and scalable operations. Recognizing the true cost of inadequate facilities is crucial for building a distribution network that supports growth and maximizes profitability.

Chapter 7:

Overlooking the Human Element and Essential Infrastructure: Hidden Costs in Labor and Logistics

Your warehouse operation is ultimately driven by people. Neglecting the basic needs of your employees and logistical partners can lead to significant hidden costs in productivity, morale, and overall efficiency.

Think about your warehouse from the perspective of your staff and the truck drivers who service your facility. Are their basic needs being met? Is the infrastructure in place to allow them to perform their jobs effectively?

The Human Cost of Neglect

- Conveyance Challenges for Staff: If your warehouse is in a location with limited public transportation, employees may face difficult commutes. This can lead to:
    - High Turnover: It's harder to attract and retain reliable labor, increasing recruitment and training costs.
    - Increased Absenteeism: Unreliable transport can lead to lateness and absence, disrupting schedules and reducing productivity.
    - Lower Morale: Frustration with commuting can negatively impact employee morale and focus.

- Company Transport Costs: In severe cases, you may have to provide company-sponsored transport, adding a significant operational cost.

Ignoring the Needs of Your Logistics Partners

- Insufficient Truck Parking and Loading Bays: A lack of adequate parking creates congestion and delays. Insufficient loading bays lead to longer turnaround times, which can incur demurrage and detention charges and make your facility less appealing to carriers.
- Lack of Basic Amenities: Failing to provide clean restrooms and washrooms for staff and drivers is not just a matter of common decency; it's a fundamental requirement for a functional work environment. The absence of these facilities leads to:
  - Poor Morale and Productivity: Lack of comfort impacts morale and can decrease productivity.
  - Driver Dissatisfaction: Drivers are more likely to prefer facilities with amenities, and neglecting their needs can make it harder to secure reliable transportation.

Investing in People and Infrastructure Pays Off

Neglecting the human element and essential infrastructure can create significant friction, reduce productivity, and ultimately erode your profitability. Investing in solutions like transportation options for staff, sufficient parking, and clean amenities is a strategic move that leads to a more efficient, productive, and profitable distribution warehouse.

Potential Financial Losses

The combined impact of neglecting these crucial elements can range from 3% to 15% or more of your total annual sales revenue.

Ask yourself:

- Are long commutes affecting staff retention or productivity?
- Have transportation challenges led to higher recruitment costs or the need for company transport?
- Are trucks facing parking or maneuvering issues, causing delays?
- Are inadequate amenities affecting morale or making your location less attractive to carriers?

Conclusion

Warehouse success depends on its human element and supportive infrastructure. Neglecting details like staff conveyance or driver amenities leads to significant profit drains through high turnover, reduced productivity, and strained carrier relationships. Investing in your team's well-being directly enhances efficiency, reliability, and financial performance.

Chapter 8:

Optimizing Your Warehouse Layout: The Foundation of Efficient Operations

Beyond structural issues and accessibility, a well-planned internal layout is paramount to maximizing warehouse efficiency and minimizing waste. A disorganized layout, with haphazardly stored materials and undefined areas, can lead to a cascade of negative consequences that erode profitability.

The High Cost of Chaos: The Impact of a Poorly Planned Layout

A disorganized warehouse leads to a multitude of problems:

- Reduced Storage Capacity: Without a systematic approach, you waste valuable space. Cluttered aisles and inefficient stacking result in lower storage density and may force you to seek a larger, more expensive warehouse.
- Increased Time and Labor Costs: Staff spend more time searching for items, increasing labor costs and slowing order fulfilment.
- Increased Fatigue and Reduced Productivity: Navigating a chaotic environment is physically and mentally demanding, leading to increased fatigue and lower morale.

- Higher Risk of Accidents: Cluttered aisles and obstructed pathways create safety hazards, increasing the risk of accidents and injuries.
- Inventory Management Challenges: Without a systematic layout, accurate inventory tracking is difficult, leading to stockouts, overstocking, and errors.
- Increased Errors and Mis-shipments: In a chaotic environment, it's easy to pick the wrong items or mis-ship orders, leading to increased costs and customer dissatisfaction.

Designing for Efficiency: Key Elements of a Well-Planned Layout

A well-planned layout creates a streamlined, efficient, and safe environment. Key elements include:

- Clearly Marked and Designated Areas: Define specific zones for:
  - Receiving (Goods Inward)
  - Shipping (Goods Outward)
  - Checking and Packing
  - Storage for Non-Billed Stock
  - Damaged Material Area
  - Sales Return Area
  - Office Area

- Fire Extinguishers and Safety Equipment
- Aisle Space between Racks
- Parking for Material Handling Equipment
- Washroom Facilities

- Optimized Storage Systems: Choose the right racking, shelving, or pallet systems based on the type, size, and quantity of goods.
- Efficient Material Flow: Design the layout to minimize travel distances and optimize the flow of materials from receiving to shipping.
- Clear Signage and Labelling: Use clear and consistent signage to help staff easily locate items and navigate the warehouse.
- Safety Considerations: Incorporate safety features like designated pedestrian walkways and guardrails.

Potential Financial Losses

The combined impact of an inefficient layout can range from 2% to 8% of your total annual sales revenue, especially for businesses with high throughput or complex product mixes.

Ask yourself:

- Does staff often walk-through cluttered aisles looking for items, leading to accidents?
- Do you experience frequent stockouts or mis-shipments due to difficulty tracking inventory?

- What is the potential cost of expanding your warehouse versus optimizing your current layout?

Conclusion

By proactively embracing a well-designed layout, you unlock hidden capacity, boost productivity, reduce costly errors and accidents, and ultimately fortify your business against inefficiencies.

Chapter 9:

Investing in the Right Physical Storage and Handling Infrastructure: The Engine of Operational Efficiency

Beyond a well-planned layout, the physical infrastructure you use for storing and handling goods is critical to your warehouse's efficiency and profitability. Choosing the right equipment and storage systems can significantly impact space utilization, material flow, labour costs, and safety.

Key Elements of an Efficient Physical Infrastructure

- Strategic Vertical Storage with Heavy-Duty Racking: To maximize cubic space, invest in appropriate heavy-duty racking systems. The best choice depends on your inventory characteristics and accessibility needs:
    - Selective Pallet Racking: Best for diverse inventory; allows direct access to every pallet.
    - Drive-In/Drive-Thru Racking: Ideal for high-volume, low-SKU items, maximizing storage density.
    - Push-Back Racking: Offers higher density while still allowing for multiple SKUs.
    - Cantilever Racking: Designed for long or bulky items.
    - Multi-Tier Racking: Creates multiple levels of storage, using vertical space.

- Optimized Aisle Space: The width of your aisles must balance accessibility and storage density. The choice depends on your equipment:
    - Counterbalance Forklifts: Require wider aisles (10-13 feet).
    - Reach Trucks: Operate in narrower aisles (8-10 feet), improving storage density.
    - Very Narrow Aisle (VNA) Trucks: Operate in very narrow aisles (around 6 feet), significantly increasing capacity.
- Standardized Material Handling with Quality Pallets: Using good-quality, standardized wooden pallets provides a stable and uniform base. Ensure they are the correct size and strength for your equipment and loads, and are regularly inspected.

- Efficient Internal Movement: For short distances, a reliable hand-operated pallet.
- Trucks are indispensable. For stacking at lower levels, stackers offer a cost-effective solution.

- The Lifting Power of Forklifts: Forklifts are the backbone of vertical movement and heavy loads. When choosing, consider:
  - Power Source: Electric for indoor use, internal combustion for outdoor or well-ventilated areas.
  - Lifting Capacity and Height: Ensure the forklift can safely handle your maximum weight to the highest racking levels.
  - Manoeuvrability: Select models appropriate for your aisle widths and layout.

Potential Financial Losses

- Poor Storage Infrastructure: 1.0% - 5.0% of annual sales.
- Wrong Material Handling Infrastructure: 1.5% - 5.0% of annual sales.

Ask yourself:

- Are we using the right racking, aisle widths, and storage methods to optimize space and equipment efficiency?
- Is our material handling equipment suitable, safe, and cost-effective for smooth operations?

Conclusion

The physical storage and handling infrastructure is the operational engine of your warehouse. A deliberate choice of appropriate heavy-duty racking, optimized aisle spaces, quality pallets, and the right mix of material handling equipment is not an expense but a strategic imperative. This drives higher productivity, reduced damage, enhanced safety, and ultimately, a more robust and profitable supply chain.

Investing in Your Warehouse is Investing in Your Future with Compounding Returns and a Competitive Edge

Investing in a warehouse's location, specifications, layout, and infrastructure isn't just an expense; it's a strategic investment that generates compounding returns for your business's future success and profitability.

From 1999 to 2025, I was a prisoner in my own business. My family's company, a legacy built on hard work and dedication, was a constant struggle. For decades, our business ran on a "person-based" system, not a "process-based" one. This meant that everything depended on me, and I was always in firefighting mode. My days were a blur of solving problems, a relentless cycle that left no time for my family, friends, or even my own well-being.

I was living in a state of constant burnout, and the business was stagnating. We hired an HR consultant in 2019 who gave us job descriptions (JDs), but they were so complex that they ended up gathering dust in a cupboard. We couldn't measure performance, identify our best employees, or hold anyone accountable. The business was running on hope and luck, a "push-based" system where I had to constantly push things forward.

Everything changed in 2022 when my friends, Mr. Niket Singania and Mr. Ravindra Patil, introduced me to business coach Mr. Rahul Jain. Under his guidance, we transformed our operations. We created clear job descriptions and a system to measure the performance of every team member. It was a difficult transition, but the results were undeniable.

Today, on August 5, 2025, I'm proud to say that my business is a "pull-based" system. My team's performance is over 50% higher, and I know exactly who my top performers are. The business runs on a smooth, process-based system, freeing up my time to focus on strategic growth. I've broken free from the firefighting cycle and am now able to enjoy a fulfilling life outside of work. This journey taught me a vital lesson: a business must run on process, not on people. It's the only way to achieve true freedom and sustainable growth.

B

The Inefficiency Trap: From Person-Based to Process-Based Operations

While a dedicated workforce is essential, relying on individual workers' methods rather than standardized processes creates a significant drag on a warehouse's efficiency and profitability. This "person-based" approach, where success depends on who is doing the work rather than how it's done, becomes a major impediment to growth.

Chapter 10:

The Hidden Costs of Person-Based Operations

Inconsistency and Variability: Relying on individual methods leads to inconsistent performance, making it difficult to maintain standards for speed, accuracy, and quality. This makes it challenging to predict output and meet deadlines.

Susceptibility to Human Error: Repetitive tasks under pressure are prone to human error, which results in costly mis-shipments, inventory discrepancies, and a damaged reputation.

Limited Scalability: Person-based operations are difficult to scale. As order volumes increase, adding more people increases labor costs and management complexity without a proportional increase in efficiency.

Difficulty in Tracking and Measurement: Without standardized processes, it is difficult to track performance and gather meaningful data. This prevents you from identifying bottlenecks and driving continuous improvement.

Increased Training Costs and Time: Person-based systems often require extensive on-the-job training, which is time-consuming and inefficient. High employee turnover exacerbates this problem.

Vulnerability to Disruptions: Critical knowledge resides with specific individuals, creating a "single point of failure." If a key employee is absent, operations can be significantly disrupted.

Limited Automation Potential: Person-based processes are difficult to automate. This causes you to miss out on the benefits of technology, such as increased speed, reduced errors, and improved accuracy.

Potential Financial Losses

The combined impact of these inefficiencies and high employee turnover can range from 3% to 10% of your total annual sales revenue.

Ask yourself:

- Can new staff quickly perform tasks using clear processes, or do we rely too much on individuals and informal training?
- Are we tracking performance and error costs well enough to scale operations without slowdown or over-reliance on key people?

Conclusion

Relying too heavily on person-based operations creates a system that is inconsistent, error-prone, difficult to scale, and resistant to automation. These inefficiencies silently erode your profitability and hinder your ability to compete effectively. The transition to process-based operations is a fundamental shift that is essential for long-term success.

Chapter 11:

From Individual Effort to Systemic Efficiency: A Roadmap to Process-Based Operations

Shifting from a person-based to a process-based warehouse model is crucial for profitability and scalability. This strategic transformation involves a systematic approach to standardizing operations and empowering your team.

Define Roles and Responsibilities: Create detailed job descriptions that specify the purpose of each role, key tasks, performance standards, and the frequency of task execution. This clarity ensures accountability and provides a foundation for performance evaluation.

Checklist - Warehouse

Name	Task ID	Freq	Task	Planned	Actual
Depot Incharge	253	Q	Stock Check	05-03-23 23:59	05-03-23 17:24
Depot Incharge	7	M	Internet Bill payment	16-05-23 23:59	16-05-23 10:18
DEO	20	D	Attendence	18-05-23 11:29	18-05-23 10:23
DEO	121	D	MIS Report	18-05-23 10:29	18-05-23 10:18
Supervisor	258	D	Sweeping	18-05-23 10:15	18-05-23 10:31
Supervisor	216	W	Water Dispancer cleaning	10-07-23 23:59	
Depot Incharge	4	M	Electricity Bill Pyament	20-05-23 23:59	20-05-23 13:07
Depot Incharge	11	M	Catridge refilling	25-05-23 23:59	24-05-23 10:16
Depot Incharge	14	M	Order Thermal Lable	25-05-23 23:59	25-05-23 13:27
Depot Incharge	1	M	Customer Bills	03-05-23 23:59	05-05-23 10:33
Depot Incharge	255	M	Cash Statement	03-05-23 23:59	05-05-23 11:42
Supervisor	115	M	Racks Cleaning	04-06-23 23:59	
Supervisor	118	M	Air Cooler Cleaning	04-06-23 23:59	
DEO	241	M	Cupboad & DVR Box cleaning	06-06-23 23:59	
Supervisor	247	M	Fire Extenguisher Cleaning	07-06-23 23:59	
Supervisor	353	M	Cobweb cleaning	08-06-23 23:59	

© Esteem Groups 2022 | Esteem Confidential

Esteem Integrated Logistic (P) Ltd | Esteem Trucking Company | Esteem Bio Fuel (P) Ltd | Esteem Vehicle Carriers

Checklist - Warehouse Incharge

Name	Task ID	Freq	Task	Planned	Actual
Incharge	301	D	Wearhouse Floor Cleaning (Bay1)	01-01-2024	01-09-2024
Incharge	1861	M	Racks Cleaning	05-01-2024	01-09-2024
Incharge	1873	M	Air Cooler Cleaning	05-01-2024	01-09-2024
Incharge	1885	M	Cupboad & DVR Box cleaning	04-01-2024	01-09-2024
Incharge	1897	M	Fire Extenguisher Cleaning	03-01-2024	01-09-2024
Incharge	1933	M	Water Dispancer cleaning	05-01-2024	01-09-2024

Esteem Integrated Logistic (P) Ltd | Esteem Trucking Company | Esteem Bio Fuel (P) Ltd | Esteem Vehicle Carriers

Checklist - Warehouse Supervisor

Name	Task ID	Freq	Task	Planned	Actual
Supervisor	901	D	Daily MIS	01-01-2024	01-09-2024
Supervisor	1201	D	Perpetual Inventory	01-01-2024	01-09-2024
Supervisor	1501	D	Space Utilization Report	01-01-2024	01-09-2024
Supervisor	1801	M	Customer Bills	03-01-2024	01-08-2024
Supervisor	1813	M	Electricity Bill Pyament	16-01-2024	1/16/2024
Supervisor	1825	M	Internet Bill payment	16-01-2024	1/16/2024
Supervisor	1837	M	Catridge refilling	25-01-2024	02-07-2024
Supervisor	1849	M	Provision Mail	05-01-2024	01-08-2024
Supervisor	1909	M	Cash Statement	03-01-2024	01-08-2024
Supervisor	1921	M	Cobweb cleaning	05-01-2024	01-09-2024
Supervisor	1945	Y	UPS Service	10-09-2024	9/13/2024
Supervisor	1953	Y	Bell Scale renewal	01-06-2024	06-12-2024
Supervisor	1957	Y	Fire Extenguisher renewal	01-10-2024	10-01-2024
Supervisor	1961	Y	Trollys Service	01-10-2024	10-01-2024
Supervisor	1965	M	Stock Check	05-01-2024	01-09-2024
Supervisor	1977	Q	Office Earthing	05-03-2024	03-06-2024
Supervisor	1981	Q	Rolling shetter greasing	05-03-2024	03-06-2024

© Esteem Groups 2022 | Esteem Confidential

Esteem Integrated Logistic (P) Ltd | Esteem Trucking Company | Esteem Bio Fuel (P) Ltd | Esteem Vehicle Carriers

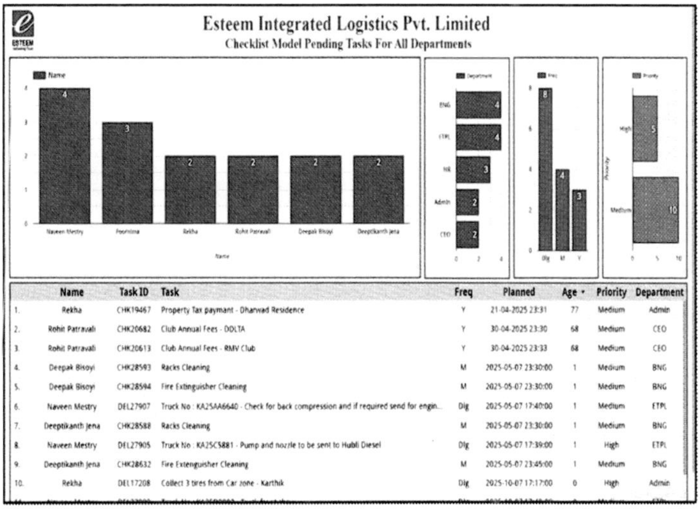

Visualize the Workflow: Develop flowcharts to map out all key warehouse processes (e.g., receiving, picking, shipping). This visual representation helps identify bottlenecks, eliminate redundancies, and improve coordination between teams.

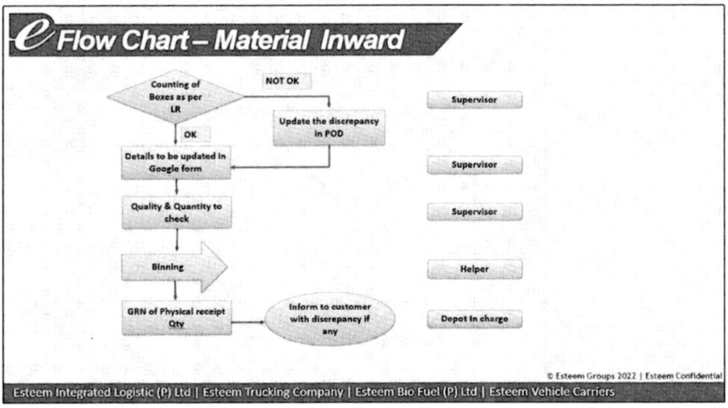

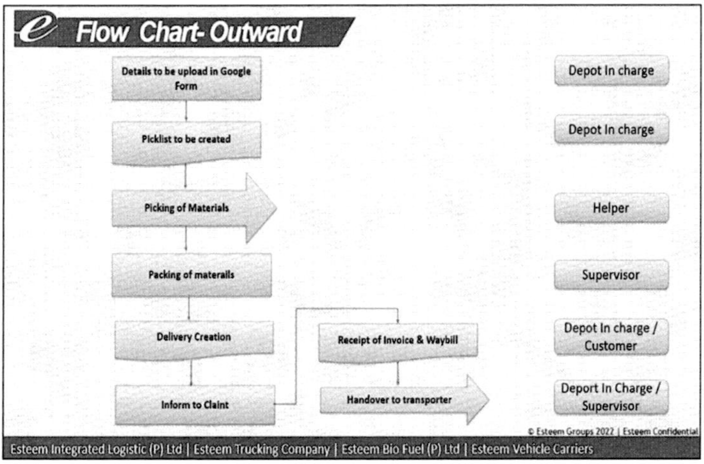
Flow Chart- Outward
Details to be upload in Google Form
Picklist to be created
Picking of Materials
Packing of materails
Delivery Creation
Inform to Claint
Receipt of Invoice & Waybill
Handover to transporter
Depot In charge
Depot In charge
Helper
Supervisor
Depot In charge / Customer
Deport In Charge / Supervisor
© Esteem Groups 2022 | Esteem Confidential
Esteem Integrated Logistic (P) Ltd | Esteem Trucking Company | Esteem Bio Fuel (P) Ltd | Esteem Vehicle Carriers

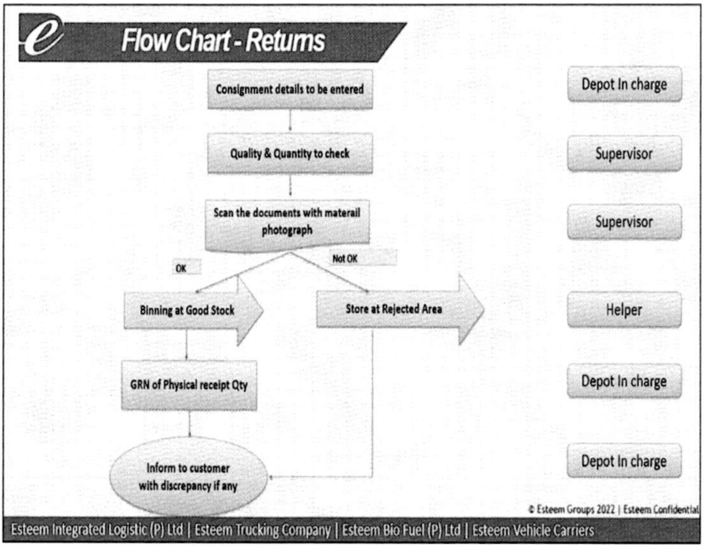
Flow Chart - Returns
Consignment details to be entered
Quality & Quantity to check
Scan the documents with materail photograph
OK
Not OK
Binning at Good Stock
Store at Rejected Area
GRN of Physical receipt Qty
Inform to customer with discrepancy if any
Depot In charge
Supervisor
Supervisor
Helper
Depot In charge
Depot In charge
© Esteem Groups 2022 | Esteem Confidential
Esteem Integrated Logistic (P) Ltd | Esteem Trucking Company | Esteem Bio Fuel (P) Ltd | Esteem Vehicle Carriers

Measure Performance: Conduct time and motion studies to establish a baseline for how long each task should take. This data allows you to set realistic performance targets, standardize work methods, and identify areas for improvement.

Standardize Procedures: Create Standard Operating Procedures (SOPs) and comprehensive operating manuals. SOPs provide step-by-step instructions for tasks, while manuals offer a broader overview of warehouse operations, ensuring consistent execution and effective training.

Empower Your Team with Training: Invest in training videos that visually demonstrate new processes, explain their benefits, and provide instructions on how to use new tools. This ensures consistent training delivery and improves knowledge retention.

Leverage Technology: Implement a task measurement application to track key performance indicators (KPIs) like picking rates and order fulfilment times. This provides real-time visibility and the data needed to make informed decisions and drive continuous improvement.

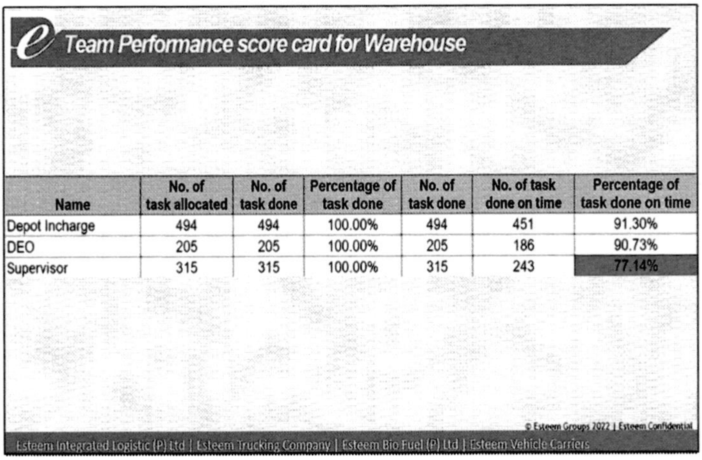

Name	No. of task allocated	No. of task done	Percentage of task done	No. of task done	No. of task done on time	Percentage of task done on time
Depot Incharge	494	494	100.00%	494	451	91.30%
DEO	205	205	100.00%	205	186	90.73%
Supervisor	315	315	100.00%	315	243	77.14%

Drive Continuous Improvement: Establish a culture of ongoing optimization by regularly reviewing data, soliciting employee feedback, and making adjustments to processes. This ensures your operations remain efficient and adaptable.

The Result: A Process-Based Transformation

This structured approach leads to a warehouse that is efficient, consistent, measurable, scalable, safer, and more profitable. This transformation can boost annual sales revenue (or reduce equivalent costs) by 3% to 10%.

Ask Yourself:

- Are roles and processes clearly documented and easy to follow?
- Do we track task times and use that data to improve operations?

Conclusion

Transitioning to process-based operations is a significant investment that yields substantial and long-lasting returns, building a system that empowers employees and drives sustainable success.

Chapter 12:

Retaining Top Talent: Building a Culture of Value and Growth

Retaining good employees is crucial for warehouse operations. High turnover is costly and disruptive. To foster loyalty and motivate your team, consider these strategies:

1. Competitive Compensation and Benefits: Offer competitive wages, essential benefits, and promise growth opportunities with regular increments.

2. Performance Incentives and Profit Sharing: Implement performance-based bonuses and profit-sharing to motivate employees, foster ownership, and align their goals with the company's.

3. Opportunities for Growth and Development: Invest in training and mentorship programs to help employees develop new skills.

4. A Positive and Supportive Work Environment: Foster a culture of open communication, teamwork, and collaboration.

5. Empowerment and Autonomy: Delegate responsibility and allow employees to make decisions, giving them a sense of ownership.

6. Strong Leadership and Management: Ensure managers embody company values, communicate expectations clearly, and offer support.

Positive Financial Impact

Implementing these strategies can lead to a net positive financial impact of 2% to 7% (or higher) of your annual sales revenue by increasing productivity and reducing costs.

Ask yourself:

- Are we rewarding staff fairly through pay, bonuses, and growth opportunities based on performance and potential?
- Do we empower employees by listening to their input and ensuring managers lead with clarity, support, and fairness?

Conclusion

By integrating perks, incentives, and profit sharing, along with other retention strategies, you can create a high-performing and stable workforce that drives loyalty, performance, and sustainable success.

C

Taming the Inventory Beast: From Profit Killer to Profit Generator

When I visit a customer's warehouse, I'm often shocked by what I see. Goods are stored in a messy way, and I wonder how they even keep track of their inventory. How do they follow FIFO (First-In, First-Out), a key rule for managing stock? The truth is, they don't. Their storage is disorganized, and products are often damaged because they are just lying on the floor or in the walking aisles. It's heart breaking to see good stock get ruined like this.

I also notice that there's no proper process for sending out materials. It makes me worry that things like theft or other wrongdoings might be happening. A major risk I see is that many warehouses are completely dependent on the warehouse in charge. If that person quits, the entire business operation can come to a standstill, leaving the owner in a desperate situation.

Inventory losses are one of the biggest reasons for business failure. This is because, in many cases, I see that they use Excel sheets or Tally to manage their stock. The problem with Excel is that anyone can change the data without a trace, so you never know if the numbers are correct. Because the owner doesn't have a clear idea of what stock they have, they end up buying more material than needed, just to be safe. This locks up their money and fills up their already crowded warehouse.

All these poor practices lead to heavy financial losses from damaged goods, missing stock, and theft. Sometimes, the team can't even find the right items to dispatch, so they send out incomplete orders. This makes customers unhappy and costs the company more money in extra transport fees.

The root of all this mess is a lack of a proper warehouse setup. There are no clear processes, no one is held accountable, and no technology is used to help. Business owners need to stop seeing their warehouse as just a storage space and start investing in good infrastructure, storage systems, and technology. This is the only way to protect their capital and ensure their business grows.

Chapter 13:

The Perils of Poor Inventory Management: A Recipe for Financial Disaster

In the distribution business, inventory is the lifeblood, the very asset you sell to generate revenue. However, if not managed with precision, it can quickly turn from a valuable asset into a major liability, silently draining your profits and threatening the survival of your business. This chapter will explore the various ways poor inventory management can harm your business and provide a roadmap for transforming inventory into a profit generator.

Poorly managed inventory can devastate your bottom line in numerous and often hidden ways.

The High Cost of Excess Inventory

Holding more stock than you need is a drain on resources.

1. Capital Blockage: Every rupee tied up in excess inventory is capital that cannot be used for other critical investments, such as marketing, expansion, or debt reduction. This directly impacts your company's liquidity and growth potential.
2. Storage Costs: Excess inventory requires more storage space, leading to increased warehousing costs, including rent, utilities, insurance, and security.

3. Interest Payments: If you've borrowed money to finance your inventory, you'll incur interest payments on the excess stock, further eroding your profits.
4. Obsolescence and Expiry: Products, especially those with short shelf lives or subject to market trends, can become obsolete or expire if held for too long. This results in write-offs and significant losses, as the inventory can no longer be sold at full value.

The Pitfalls of Insufficient Inventory

The opposite problem, not having enough stock, is just as damaging.

1. Lost Sales: Running out of stock when customers demand it leads to immediate lost sales opportunities and revenue loss.
2. Customer Dissatisfaction: Stockouts frustrate customers, damage your reputation, and can drive them to your competitors, often permanently.
3. Damage to Brand Image: Consistent stockouts can create the impression that your business is unreliable and inefficient, eroding trust and long-term brand value.

The Importance of Optimal Inventory

The key is not to have every SKU in stock at all times, but to strategically stock items that are most valuable to your business. This involves focusing on products with high gross profit (GP) and those that are fast-selling with high turnover rates. By prioritizing these items, you can maximize profitability while minimizing holding costs.

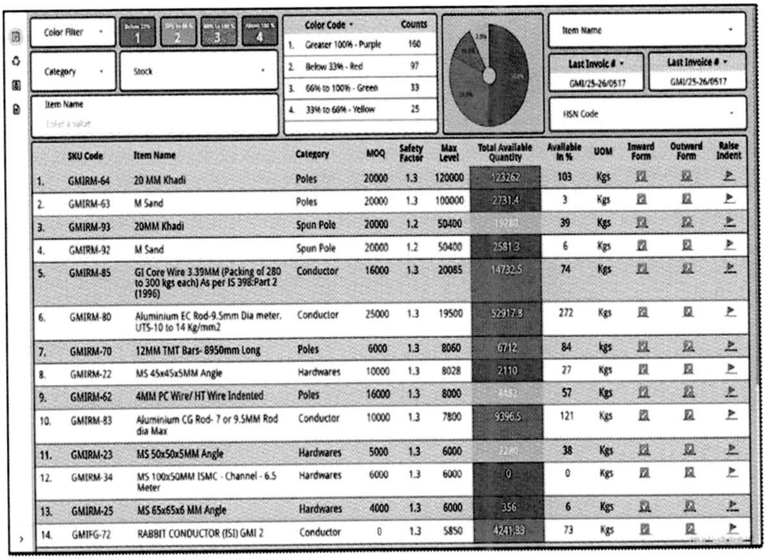

	SKU Code	Item Name	Category	MOQ	Safety Factor	Max Level	Total Available Quantity	Available In %	UOM	Inward Form	Outward Form	Raise Indent
1.	GMIRM-64	20 MM Khadi	Poles	20000	1.3	120000	123262	103	Kgs			
2.	GMIRM-63	M Sand	Poles	20000	1.3	100000	2731.4	3	Kgs			
3.	GMIRM-93	20MM Khadi	Spun Pole	20000	1.2	50400	[illegible]	39	Kgs			
4.	GMIRM-92	M Sand	Spun Pole	20000	1.2	50400	2581.3	6	Kgs			
5.	GMIRM-85	GI Core Wire 3.39MM (Packing of 280 to 300 kgs each) As per IS 398:Part 2 (1996)	Conductor	16000	1.3	20085	14732.5	74	Kgs			
6.	GMIRM-80	Aluminium EC Rod-9.5mm Dia meter, UTS-10 to 14 Kg/mm2	Conductor	25000	1.3	19500	52917.8	272	Kgs			
7.	GMIRM-70	12MM TMT Bars- 8950mm Long	Poles	6000	1.3	8060	6712	84	kgs			
8.	GMIRM-22	MS 45x45x5MM Angle	Hardwares	10000	1.3	8028	2110	27	Kgs			
9.	GMIRM-62	4MM PC Wire/ HT Wire Indented	Poles	16000	1.3	8000	[illegible]	57	Kgs			
10.	GMIRM-83	Aluminium CG Rod- 7 or 9.5MM Rod dia Max	Conductor	10000	1.3	7800	9396.5	121	Kgs			
11.	GMIRM-23	MS 50x50x5MM Angle	Hardwares	5000	1.3	6000	[illegible]	38	Kgs			
12.	GMIRM-34	MS 100x50MM ISMC - Channel - 6.5 Meter	Hardwares	6000	1.3	6000	0	0	Kgs			
13.	GMIRM-25	MS 65x65x6 MM Angle	Hardwares	4000	1.3	6000	356	6	Kgs			
14.	GMIFG-72	RABBIT CONDUCTOR (ISI) GMI 2	Conductor	0	1.3	5850	4241.83	73	Kgs			

The Scourge of Storage Losses

Inventory can be lost or damaged within the warehouse itself. This "shrinkage" can occur due to:

1. Storage Damage: Improper handling, stacking, or environmental factors.
2. Theft: Both internal and external theft can be a significant problem.
3. Errors: Mistakes such as shipping more than a customer ordered (excess dispatch) or sending products with incorrect pricing (wrong MRP dispatch) directly reduce your available stock.
4. Wrong SKU Dispatch: Shipping the wrong item to a customer leads to returns and increased logistical costs.

5. Pest Damage: Rodents and other pests can contaminate or damage products, leading to a total loss of the inventory.

The Perils of Inaccurate Inventory Records

Any discrepancy between your physical inventory and your records indicates a problem. This mismatch makes it impossible to make informed decisions about ordering, pricing, and sales. Causes of these discrepancies include:

1. Data entry errors.
2. Inefficient or inaccurate receiving and shipping processes.
3. Lack of regular cycle counts to verify stock levels.

The Inadequacy of Spreadsheets and Accounting Software

Relying on tools like Excel or basic accounting software like Tally for inventory management is a critical mistake. These tools are prone to manual errors, lack real-time visibility, and do not have the advanced features needed for optimal inventory control, such as automated replenishment, location tracking, and integration with modern warehouse technology.

The Owner's Role: A Daily Inventory Check-Up

While a Warehouse Management System (WMS) provides the tools for effective inventory management, the business owner must take an active role in reviewing its performance. A dedicated 30-minute daily review is crucial for making strategic decisions. This check-up should focus on:

- Stock levels of key SKUs: Identifying potential stockouts or overstock situations.
- Inventory turnover: Monitoring how quickly inventory is selling to identify slow-moving items.
- Order fulfilment rates: Tracking the percentage of orders that are fulfilled on time and in full.
- Discrepancy and backorder reports: Investigating the root causes of any inventory mismatches and addressing backordered items.

A key focus of this daily review should be on increasing inventory turnover, a measure of how efficiently a business is using its inventory. A higher turnover rate indicates better management and stronger sales. Strategies to improve this include optimizing pricing, improving demand forecasting, and streamlining order fulfilment processes.

Overall Potential Financial Losses

Poor inventory management can lead to substantial financial losses, collectively estimated to range from 2% to 10% of your total annual sales revenue. These losses stem from both having too much and too little stock, compounded by physical losses and data inaccuracies.

Ask Yourself:

- How accurate is your inventory, and what are the financial costs of shrinkage, stockouts, and discrepancies?

- Is your capital unnecessarily tied up in excess or obsolete stock?
- Do you have effective processes for cycle counts and returns, and what is their impact on your operations and costs?
- Are you currently tracking inventory and managing stock in an organized manner?
- Do you have a system to identify and minimize losses from excess inventory, theft, or damage?
- Do you use modern inventory management systems, or are you still relying on spreadsheets?

Conclusion

By combining the power of a WMS with proactive ownership and a focus on inventory turnover, distribution businesses can transform inventory from a major source of potential losses into a powerful driver of profitability. Mastering inventory is about optimizing cash flow, enhancing customer satisfaction, and ensuring every item is a strategic asset, making it a cornerstone of your profit engine.

Chapter 14:
Leveraging Technology for Warehouse Efficiency

In today's fast-paced distribution landscape, technology is no longer a luxury but a critical necessity for efficient warehouse operations. Implementing the right software applications and hardware can significantly streamline processes, improve accuracy, enhance visibility, and drive overall profitability. This chapter explores the key technological components that can transform your warehouse from a cost centre into a powerful competitive advantage.

Key Software and Hardware for Modern Warehouses

To run an efficient modern warehouse, you need the right technology. These specialized software applications and hardware act as the backbone of your operations, managing everything from when products arrive to when they are shipped. By automating tasks and providing real-time data, this technology helps you handle more work, reduce errors, and make smarter business decisions. The following sections will detail the essential software applications that make a warehouse high-performing

Here are some of the essential software applications and technologies used in modern warehouse operations:

1. Warehouse Management System (WMS): The WMS is the backbone of modern warehouse operations, providing comprehensive control and real-time visibility over a wide range of processes. Its core functions are designed to automate and optimize every step of the warehouse workflow.

- Real-time Inventory Tracking: It provides up-to-the-minute visibility into the stock levels, location, and status of every product in your warehouse. This allows for accurate stock counts and prevents overstocking or stockouts.
- Automated Replenishment: Based on sales data and predefined rules, the WMS helps determine optimal order quantities and automatically generates purchase orders to suppliers, ensuring you have enough stock without holding excess inventory.
- Efficient Receiving and Put-Away: The system streamlines the receiving process by using barcode scanning and automated data capture. This ensures that inventory is accurately recorded and directs staff to the most efficient storage location.
- Optimized Picking and Packing: The WMS optimizes picking routes for staff, reducing travel time and errors. It can also manage different picking methods, such as batch picking or zone picking, to maximize speed and efficiency.
- Comprehensive Reporting and Analytics: A WMS provides valuable data on key performance indicators (KPIs) like

inventory turnover, order fulfilment rates, and labor productivity, allowing you to make data-driven decisions.

2. Inventory Management System (IMS): While often a component of a WMS, a dedicated IMS can offer more specialized functions. It typically focuses on demand forecasting to predict future customer demand, order management to streamline the order-to-fulfilment cycle, and inventory optimization to analyse data and set ideal safety stock levels and reorder points.
3. Task Measurement Applications: These applications are essential for measuring and improving team performance. They track KPIs like picking rates, put-away times, and order processing times, providing data to identify bottlenecks, optimize workflows, and improve labor productivity. This data-driven approach to performance management moves away from subjective assessment to objective, actionable insights.
4. Barcode Scanning Systems: Barcode technology is a foundational element for accurate and efficient data capture. Barcode scanners are used for:

- Receiving and Put-Away: Scanning incoming goods to automatically update inventory records.
- Picking and Packing: Scanning products during the picking process to ensure accuracy and reduce errors.
- Inventory Tracking: Tracking the movement of inventory within the warehouse.
- Cycle Counting: Quickly and accurately counting inventory to reconcile system records. The use of barcode scanners

significantly reduces manual data entry, minimizes errors, and speeds up warehouse operations.

5. Other Key Technologies:

- Radio Frequency Identification (RFID): An advanced technology that uses electronic tags to track inventory in real-time without needing a direct line of sight. This is especially useful for high-value or high-volume goods where speed and accuracy are paramount.
- Transportation Management Systems (TMS): A TMS, when integrated with warehouse systems, helps manage the inbound and outbound movement of goods. It optimizes routes, tracks shipments, and reduces transportation costs, indirectly enhancing warehouse efficiency.

Selecting the right software for your warehouse is a critical decision that can have a long-lasting impact on your operations. The choice should be a strategic one, based on a careful evaluation of your specific needs and long-term goals. Here are the key factors to consider in more detail:

- Size and Complexity: The scale of your business and the complexity of your processes are primary drivers. A small warehouse with a simple workflow needs a different solution than a large-scale distribution center with high order volumes.
- Nature of Your Products: The type of products you handle, such as perishable goods or high-value items, will influence the features you need in your software.

- Your Budget: Conduct a thorough cost-benefit analysis. Consider the initial purchase price, implementation costs, training, and ongoing maintenance fees to find a solution that fits your budget.
- Your Growth Plans: Choose a system that is scalable and can handle increased transaction volumes, additional locations, and new product lines as your business expands.

The Importance of Integration

Regardless of the specific applications you choose, seamless integration between all your systems is crucial. Integrated systems allow for a smooth flow of data, eliminate redundancies, and provide a holistic, real-time view of your entire operation, from receiving to shipping.

Overall Potential Financial Losses Due to Non-Leveraging of Technology

Failing to implement these key warehouse technologies can result in substantial financial losses, often ranging from 4% to 15% of your total annual sales revenue. These losses are a direct result of inefficiencies, errors, and a lack of critical insights that technology is designed to prevent.

Ask Yourself:

- Are you using your technology effectively? Do you fully utilize your WMS and other applications, or are you only using basic features? A significant investment is only worthwhile when its features are fully adopted.

- Are manual processes or poor integration slowing you down? Identify any outdated manual processes or systems that don't communicate with each other. These issues lead to delays, errors, and a lack of real-time visibility.
- Is your technology ready for the future? Assess if your systems can scale with your business and integrate with new technologies. Ensure your staff is well-trained to use the tools and that you have a plan for future technology reviews.

Conclusion

Adopting the right technology is no longer an option but a critical imperative for warehouse efficiency and survival. From the foundational control offered by a WMS to the precision of barcode scanning and the insights from task measurement applications, technology transforms every facet of warehouse operation. By systematically streamlining processes, enhancing accuracy, and providing invaluable data, these digital tools convert your warehouse from a potential cost center into a powerful engine of growth, significantly boosting profitability and securing a competitive edge in the market.

D

Transportation Is Never an Afterthought: Select the Right Transporter Since the Start

As a freight forwarder, I've witnessed a pattern that has always troubled me: the critical role of a reliable transporter is often the last thing on a shipper's mind. The rush to move goods often leads to sourcing vehicles from brokers and owner-drivers without a proper agreement in place. There's a dangerous assumption that a verbal agreement is enough to protect a shipment.

In this chaotic process, a fundamental step is overlooked: checking vehicle documents before loading. It's a risk most shippers take, assuming that the safe delivery of their goods is solely the transporter's responsibility. It's an easy mistake to make, especially with the common but incorrect belief that the goods are covered under the vehicle's insurance.

This misconception is where the real nightmare begins. When damage, theft, or loss occurs during transit, the harsh reality hits: the transporter is often not liable for the goods. The financial burden of the loss falls squarely on the shipper, a painful lesson learned far too late.

Over my two decades in this industry, I have seen countless truck accidents and thefts. In some of the most gut-wrenching cases, entire trucks and their valuable cargo have been hijacked and are still missing. But the most devastating part? In most of these instances, the goods were not covered by marine insurance, leaving the shipper to bear the entire staggering loss.

Even when marine insurance was in place, I have seen claims rejected because the truck lacked valid documents.

It's a devastating blow that proves a critical point: the journey of your goods is only as secure as the transporter you choose.

My experience has taught me one undeniable truth: selecting a reliable transporter is not a last-minute detail; it is the most important decision a shipper can make. It's about protecting your cargo, your business, and your peace of mind. Never let it be an afterthought.

Chapter 15:

Transportation: Mastering the Flow of Goods

In warehouse operations, transportation can be categorized into two main types: inbound transportation and outbound transportation. These categories encompass the movement of goods into and out of the warehouse, respectively.

Inbound Transportation

This refers to the movement of goods from suppliers or manufacturers to the warehouse. The primary goal is to efficiently receive materials and products to be stored.

- Supplier Deliveries: Products are delivered to the warehouse from various suppliers using trucks, vans, or other freight carriers.
- Returns: Goods returned by customers or other business partners are transported back to the warehouse for inspection, re-stocking, or disposal.
- Cross-Docking: This is a method where products are unloaded from an inbound truck and immediately loaded onto an outbound truck, minimizing storage time. The goods are not stored for a long period, which streamlines the supply chain.

Outbound Transportation

This involves the movement of goods from the warehouse to customers or other distribution centres. The goal is to ensure timely and accurate delivery to the final destination.

- Last-Mile Delivery: This is the final step in the delivery process, where a product is transported from the warehouse to the end customer's location. This is often the most expensive and time-consuming part of the supply chain.
- Wholesale Shipments: Large quantities of products are transported from the warehouse to retailers or other businesses.
- Transfer Shipments: Goods are moved between different warehouses or distribution centers within the same company to balance inventory levels

The different types of losses that can occur during the transportation of goods:

- Theft: This is a major risk, encompassing both the partial and complete loss of goods. Goods are particularly vulnerable while in transit, and incidents can also occur at warehouses and during transhipment.
- Physical Damage: This category covers a wide range of issues, including breakages and leakages that can happen due to impacts, poor handling, or improper packaging. This type of damage can occur both during the main journey and

during the process of transhipment (moving goods between trucks or from a truck to a warehouse).

- Wet Damage: This refers to damage caused by water. It can result from direct exposure to rain if the vehicle is not properly covered, or from "container rain," which is condensation that forms inside a container due to fluctuations in temperature and humidity as it moves through different climate zones.
- Accidents: Vehicle accidents, such as a truck overturning or colliding with another vehicle, can lead to significant and often total damage to the goods being transported.
- Overloading: When a vehicle is loaded beyond its weight capacity, it can cause damage to the goods because they are not properly secured. Overloading also increases the risk of accidents by compromising the vehicle's stability, handling, and braking systems.
- Mishandling: This type of damage occurs during the physical handling of goods, particularly during the loading and unloading phases. It can be caused by human error, using faulty equipment, or improper stacking, which can lead to crushing or dropping of items.

Losses from operational inefficiencies in transportation are a significant problem for distributors, impacting both profitability and customer satisfaction. The root causes often stem from poor planning and a lack of proper technology, leading to a ripple effect of increased costs and a damaged reputation.

Hiring the Wrong Vehicle

This occurs when a truck with more capacity than needed is used for a shipment. We end up paying for the truck's full rental cost, but a large portion of its space or weight capacity goes unused. This directly increases the per-unit cost of transportation and represents a significant financial waste. It also raises the risk of damage to goods, as items can shift during transit if the truck isn't properly secured.

No Route Planning & Part Load Dispatch

A lack of an optimized route plan results in drivers taking longer routes, increasing fuel consumption, and travel time. This directly contributes to delayed deliveries and a reputation for unreliability. Compounding this is the practice of part-load dispatch, where trucks are sent out before they are at full capacity. This is a less cost-effective method than a full truckload (FTL) shipment because the transportation cost is not spread across a full volume of goods. Part load shipments also have a higher risk of damage or theft, as they often require multiple stops and extra handling at transhipment hubs.

Lack of Material Traceability

This is a critical warehouse inefficiency that directly impacts transportation. When a warehouse lacks a system to accurately track where goods are stored, it can lead to multiple, fragmented dispatches to the same location. This happens because staff might mistakenly assume an item is out of stock and then find it later, requiring a second trip. This waste of time and resources not only increases transportation costs but also leads to delayed deliveries and customer dissatisfaction.

The absence of insurance during transit is an extremely serious risk. When goods are not covered by a marine or cargo insurance policy, the owner (in this case, the distributor) is solely responsible for the entire financial burden of any unforeseen incident. This means that if a truck is hijacked, a shipment is damaged in an accident, or a natural disaster occurs, the owner must absorb the complete cost of the lost or damaged material. This kind of financial hit can be devastating, directly impacting cash flow, eroding profit margins, and in some cases, threatening the very viability of the business, as it is an unexpected and often substantial loss that a company may not have the capital to withstand.

Overall Potential Financial Losses due to Transportation

The various challenges and inefficiencies in your logistics operations, encompassing inbound, outbound, and especially last-mile delivery, can lead to significant financial losses that directly eat into your total annual sales revenue. These are not just base costs of moving goods, but *avoidable* costs due to sub-optimal processes, human errors, and lack of control.

The overall potential financial losses due to logistics inefficiencies can range from approximately 3% to 12% of your total annual sales revenue.

Ask yourself:

- How are we managing and mitigating the financial risk of goods in transit, and do we have a proper insurance policy to cover theft and damage?
- What is the true cost of our transportation, and are we accurately tracking losses from issues like theft, damage, and accidents?
- Are our processes for loading, unloading, and transhipment robust enough to prevent mishandling and damage, or are these common sources of loss?
- How effectively are we optimizing our truck loads, and what is the real cost of delays from waiting for a full truck versus the expense of using smaller parcel services?
- Is our last-mile delivery process efficient and cost-effective, and how does it directly impact our customer satisfaction and overall profitability?

Conclusion

To conclude, transportation isn't just about moving goods; it's the very heartbeat of a successful warehouse and distribution business. Whether it's getting products *into* your warehouse (inbound), sending them *out* to stores (outbound), or making that crucial *final delivery* to a customer's home (last-mile), each step has its own set of challenges.

To truly succeed, you must diligently manage ever-changing transport costs, ensure your trucks are efficiently loaded, plan smart delivery routes, and always aim for on-time deliveries, while securing essential Marine Cargo Insurance for all goods while they are in transit.

If transportation isn't managed well, it can lead to significant money losses, unhappy customers, and even legal complications, ultimately stopping your business from growing. Therefore, mastering transportation is not just about logistics; it's a strategic imperative that directly impacts your profitability, customer satisfaction, and overall competitive edge.

E

The Silent Threat: Uninsured Warehouses

You see it on the news all the time, warehouses on fire, everything inside lost. But what the news doesn't tell you is the real problem: in most of these cases, the warehouse isn't insured for fire or natural disasters. The goods stored inside? They're often uninsured, too.

When a fire happens, the owner of the warehouse loses their building. The business owner who rented the space loses all their goods. The entire loss falls on them.

It's shocking to see. Businesses store millions of rupees worth of products without insurance for fire, theft, or even earthquakes. And even when they do have insurance, they often don't have enough. They value their goods for much less than they are actually worth.

A Hidden Danger: Billed Goods

Here's a crucial point most people don't know: storage insurance covers your stock, but not the items you've already sold.

Once you bill a customer for an item, it's no longer covered by that insurance. If a fire or theft happens after you've created the bill, you won't get any money for those goods. This is why it's so important to get billed items loaded onto a truck and out of the warehouse as quickly as possible.

Don't take chances with your business. It is essential to get insurance for both your warehouse and your goods. It's the only way to protect everything you've worked so hard for.

Chapter 16:

Shielding Your Assets: Essential Insurance for Warehouse Risks

A significant risk in the distribution business is that many owners fail to properly insure their goods and assets, viewing insurance premiums as an avoidable expenditure. This short-sighted perspective overlooks the primary purpose of insurance as a critical risk management tool. While a premium is a predictable and manageable cost, it serves as a strategic investment to protect against a potentially catastrophic and unpredictable loss. Without this protection, a business is left completely vulnerable to a devastating financial hit.

Key Insurance Types for Warehousing

- Fire & Property Insurance: This is the foundational protection for your fixed assets. It covers not just the cost to rebuild or repair the warehouse building, but also the machinery, racking, and other essential contents inside. It is designed to protect against a wide range of unpredictable events, including fire, lightning, explosions, natural disasters like floods and earthquakes, and man-made incidents such as theft and vandalism.

- Stock Insurance: This policy specifically covers the financial value of the goods and inventory you store in the warehouse. Your stored products are exposed to numerous risks, including fire, water damage, theft, and accidental damage from handling or equipment failure. Stock insurance ensures you are compensated for lost inventory, which protects your capital and allows you to quickly re-stock and continue operations.
- Workmen's Compensation Insurance: This is a vital and often legally mandated insurance. It provides financial support and medical coverage for employees who are injured or disabled due to work-related incidents. This is especially crucial in a high-risk warehouse environment and serves to protect the business from costly lawsuits and significant legal liabilities arising from workplace accidents.
- Marine/Transit Insurance: Also known as cargo insurance, this is essential for protecting your goods when they are not inside your warehouse. It covers inventory against a range of risks, including theft, accidental damage, and natural disasters, while they are being transported by road, rail, air, or sea. This policy ensures that your financial risk doesn't extend beyond your physical control and that you are compensated for any loss during transit.

The Financial Impact of Risks

The potential financial impact of various risks can be substantial, directly eroding profits and sales revenue.

- Fire Damage: Even a partial fire can cause a loss of 5% to 20% of your annual sales. A total fire, however, is a catastrophic event where the cost to rebuild the facility and replace all inventory can exceed 100% of your annual sales, making the business virtually unrecoverable without insurance.
- Theft (Shrinkage): Theft is a constant, quiet drain on profits, often accumulating to 0.2% to 2.0% of your annual sales revenue.
- Warehouse & Transit Damage: Damage to goods stored or in movement is a recurring cost that can add up to 0.3% to 3.0% of annual sales.

Ask Yourself:

- Does our insurance fully cover the building, equipment, stock, staff injuries, and goods in transit?
- Have we assessed worst-case risks, and are we confident our coverage would protect the business completely?

Conclusion

In a warehouse and distribution business, insurance is not just an expense; it is a fundamental pillar of risk management and business continuity. It acts as your primary defense against sudden, massive financial disasters that could easily wipe out years of hard work. By strategically and comprehensively covering your assets, the warehouse building, your inventory, your employees, and the goods in transit, you convert unpredictable and potentially business-ending risks into a manageable and predictable cost. Investing in proper insurance is a non-negotiable step toward securing the long-term safety, stability, and profitability of your business.

F

Statutory Compliance for Warehouse Businesses in India

Operating a warehouse in India requires compliance with a range of statutory licenses and registrations, which can vary by state. The following is an elaboration on the licenses you mentioned, including the purpose and general employee thresholds.

1. Rental Agreement

This is not a license but a crucial legal document. It is required as proof of address for the warehouse premises during the application for many other licenses, such as GST registration and Shops and Establishment license. It must be a legally valid agreement between the warehouse owner and the business owner.

2. Additional Place of Business (GST)

This is a registration under the Goods and Services Tax (GST) system. If your warehouse is a different location from your principal place of business, you must register it as an "additional place of business" on the GST portal. This is mandatory if your aggregate turnover exceeds the threshold limit, which is typically ₹40 lakhs for goods and ₹20 lakhs for services (with some exceptions in special category states). The number of employees is not a factor for this registration; it is based on turnover.

3. Labour License (Contract Labour)

This license is required if you engage contract labour for any work in your warehouse. It falls under the Contract Labour (Regulation and Abolition) Act, 1970.

- Purpose: To regulate the employment of contract labour and ensure their working conditions and welfare are protected.
- Employee Threshold: A Labour License is mandatory for an establishment that employs 20 or more contract labourers on any day of the preceding twelve months.

4. Shops and Commercial Establishment Act

This is a state-specific license that governs the working conditions of employees in a shop or commercial establishment, which includes warehouses.

- Purpose: To regulate working hours, rest intervals, weekly holidays, leave, and other conditions of employment.
- Employee Threshold: The requirement for this license and its applicability can vary by state. In many states, registration is required regardless of the number of employees. However, some states may have a minimum threshold, such as 10 or more employees, to trigger certain provisions of the Act.

5. Provident Fund (PF)

This falls under the Employees' Provident Funds and Miscellaneous Provisions Act, 1952.

- Purpose: To provide social security benefits to employees, including retirement savings.
- Employee Threshold: Registration with the Employees' Provident Fund Organisation (EPFO) is mandatory for any establishment that employs 20 or more employees. An

establishment with fewer than 20 employees can opt for voluntary registration.

6. Employees' State Insurance Corporation (ESIC)

This is governed by the Employees' State Insurance Act, 1948.

- Purpose: To provide employees with a comprehensive social security scheme that includes medical care, maternity benefits, and unemployment allowances.
- Employee Threshold: In most states, registration is mandatory for any establishment that employs 10 or more employees and where the employees' monthly wages are up to ₹21,000. In some states, this threshold may be 20 employees.

7. Professional Tax License

This is a state-level tax on professions, trades, and employment.

- Purpose: The employer must obtain a Professional Tax Registration Certificate (PTRC) to deduct and remit this tax from their employees' salaries to the state government.
- Employee Threshold: There is no minimum employee threshold for this. An employer must register for a Professional Tax license as soon as they hire their first employee.

8. Weights and Measurement License

This is a license required under the Legal Metrology Act, 2009.

- Purpose: This license is crucial if your warehouse uses any weighing or measuring instruments for commercial transactions, such as weighing goods for sale or charging based on weight. The license ensures that the instruments are verified, accurate, and properly sealed.
- Employee Threshold: This license is not tied to the number of employees but rather to the use of weighing and measuring instruments for commercial purposes.

Overall Potential Financial Impact Statutory Compliance

Not adhering to statutory compliance for a warehouse in India can have a significant and multifaceted financial impact on your annual sales turnover. It's not just about direct fines; it's about disruptions, lost opportunities, and damage to reputation, all of which can severely erode profitability and even lead to business closure.

Here's a breakdown of the overall financial impact, categorized by the type of consequence:

1. Direct Fines and Penalties

These are immediate financial hits imposed by regulatory bodies. They can vary greatly depending on the specific non-compliance, its severity, duration, and the governing act.

- GST Registration (Additional Place): Failure to declare an additional place of business can lead to penalties under Section 125 of the CGST/SGST Act, which allows fines up to ₹25,000 for general violations (and potentially ₹50,000 for IGST).
- Lost Input Tax Credit (ITC): This is a significant ongoing financial loss. If your warehouse is not properly declared, you might not be able to claim ITC on rent, electricity, maintenance, and other expenses incurred at that location, effectively increasing your operational costs and reducing your net profit.
- Confiscation of Goods: Goods stored or moved from an undeclared place of business might be liable for confiscation, with penalties equal to 100% of the tax or 50% of the value of goods (if the owner doesn't come forward). This is a direct loss of inventory value.

2. Shops & Commercial Establishment Act (Karnataka)

- Penalty for Non-Registration: Fines for a first offense can extend up to ₹1,000, and for subsequent offenses, up to ₹2,000. In severe cases, authorities may even shut down the establishment.
- Violations of Working Conditions: Fines can range from ₹1,000 to ₹50,000 per instance for violations related to working hours, leave policies, health, and safety standards. Repeated violations escalate penalties.
- Improper Record Keeping: Fines starting from ₹1,000 per instance.

3. Labour Licenses (Contract Labour)

- Penalty: For non-registration or contravention, the principal employer and contractor can face fines up to ₹2,00,000 (two lakh rupees), with additional fines of ₹2,000 per day for continuing contravention, potentially capped at ₹2,000 per person employed. Imprisonment up to 6 months for certain offenses is also possible.

4. PF & ESIC Registration

- Financial Penalties (Damages): Interest is charged at 12% per annum on delayed contributions. Damages (penalties) can be levied on delayed contributions, ranging from 5% for delays less than 2 months to 25% for delays over 6 months (though revised rates for EPF might cap at 12% annually as of June 2024). This applies to the *arrears* (amount not paid).
- Criminal Penalties: Imprisonment for persistent defaults (up to 1 year) or for false statements/evasion (1-3 years + fines).

5. Professional Tax Registration (Karnataka)

- Penalty for Non-Registration/Non-Enrolment: A flat penalty of ₹1,000.
- Penalty for Non-Filing of Returns: ₹250 per instance.
- Interest on Delayed Payment: Simple interest of 1.5% per month or part thereof on the due amount.
- Penalty for Non-Payment: 10% of the tax amount due (revised from 50% effective April 1, 2023).

6. Weighing Scale License

- Penalty: Using non-approved or uncalibrated instruments can result in fines starting from ₹5,000 to ₹50,000.
- Confiscation: The inaccurate devices can be seized by the administration.
- Imprisonment: In serious cases of fraudulent practice, imprisonment is also possible.

Ask Yourself:

- Is our warehouse legally registered as an "additional place of business" on the GST portal, and is our rental agreement valid and up-to-date?
- Do we have the mandatory state-specific Shops and Commercial Establishment license for our warehouse, and are our working hours and labor practices in compliance with the Act?
- Based on our current employee count, have we registered for Provident Fund (EPF) and Employees' State Insurance (ESIC) to ensure our staff receive their legal social security benefits?
- If we use contract labor, do we have the required Labour License to ensure their welfare, and if we use weighing scales, are they properly licensed under the Weights and Measurement Act?

- Do we have a system in place to stay updated on statutory changes, and have we consulted a professional to ensure we are fully compliant with all state-specific regulations?

Conclusion

In conclusion, statutory licenses for a warehouse are not just bureaucratic formalities; they are the fundamental pillars of legal and ethical business operations. By ensuring compliance with licenses for GST, labor, and social security, a business not only avoids severe penalties and legal issues but also protects its reputation and builds a stable foundation for growth. Proper licensing and compliance are essential for mitigating operational risks, safeguarding employee welfare, and ensuring that the business can operate smoothly and legitimately in the long term.

Disclaimer: Statutory requirements are subject to change and can vary significantly from one state to another. It is highly recommended to consult with a legal or business compliance professional for the most up-to-date and state-specific advice for your warehouse operations.

G

The 3-Step Profit Engine: Turning Your Warehouse into a Strategic Asset

This framework is designed to transform your warehouse from a costly center of operational inefficiencies into a profitable and strategic part of your business.

Step 1: Plug the Profit Leaks

This first step is about taking direct action to stop the financial drain caused by the seven burning areas of cash in your warehouse. By identifying and fixing these hidden errors, which are rooted in poor infrastructure, human factors, and inefficient processes, you can immediately stop unnecessary losses. This foundational step is crucial for establishing a healthy, sustainable operation that is ready for growth.

Step 2: Transition from Person-Based to Process-Based Operations

Once the profit leaks are plugged, this step focuses on building a repeatable and scalable system. The goal is to move away from relying on individual employees and create a consistent, error-resistant workflow. This is achieved through three key actions:

- Define Clear Roles: Create specific job descriptions and assign clear responsibilities for daily, weekly, and monthly tasks.
- Visualize the Workflow: Use flowcharts to map out processes like receiving and picking to easily spot and fix bottlenecks.

- Measure Performance: Establish standard times for all warehouse activities to measure performance accurately and create a baseline for future improvements.

Step 3: Strategic Focus and Outsourcing

With a loss-free and process-driven warehouse, you can now make a strategic shift. This final step involves the business owner focusing their energy on core growth areas such as strategic sourcing, sales, and marketing. Non-core functions, particularly warehousing, can be outsourced to a 3PL (Third-Party Logistics) provider. This decision, now based on a clear understanding of your costs and processes, allows you to reclaim valuable time and resources to concentrate solely on what will grow your business in the long term.

Conclusion

After identifying the "cash burning" areas in a warehouse, the decision to manage internally or outsource is a fundamental strategic choice that defines your business model. It's a question of where you believe your company's core value lies and how you want to allocate your most precious resources: time, capital, and management focus.

Option 1: Internal Management (DIY Model)

This option involves taking direct control of all seven "cash burning" areas within your warehouse. It's a high-investment, high-control strategy where you aim to build logistics into a core competency of your business.

Advantages:

- Complete Control: You have full authority over every operational detail, from staffing and processes to quality control. This allows for deep customization and quick implementation of improvements.
- Higher Profit Potential: By eliminating a 3PL's profit margin and achieving internal efficiencies, you capture all cost savings and potentially increase your overall profitability.
- Direct Visibility: You have immediate access to all data, giving you real-time insights into your operations and enabling rapid decision-making.

Disadvantages:

- High Investment & Risk: This requires significant capital for technology (WMS), equipment, and training. The risk is high; if you lack the necessary expertise, inefficiencies may persist, and the initial investment may not yield a positive return.
- Distraction from Core Business: Managing complex logistics demands a great deal of your time and attention, diverting focus from essential growth drivers like sales, marketing, and product development.

Option 2: Outsourcing to a 3PL (Third-Party Logistics)

This option involves partnering with an external company that specializes in warehousing and distribution. It's a strategic choice to leverage expert services and technology without a large capital investment.

Advantages:

- Access to Expertise & Scale: You gain immediate access to a 3PL's advanced technology, infrastructure, and skilled workforce. Their business model is based on economies of scale, offering you these benefits at a lower cost than you could achieve on your own.
- Focus on Core Business: Outsourcing frees you to concentrate on your company's primary mission, growing the business, and strengthening customer relationships.
- Cost Predictability: 3PL contracts often provide a clear, predictable cost structure, making budgeting and financial planning more straightforward.

Disadvantages:

- Loss of Direct Control: You hand over day-to-day operational control to an external partner, which can be a concern for businesses with specific needs or high-value goods.
- Risk of Poor Partnership: Your business becomes dependent on the 3PL's performance. Choosing the wrong partner can lead to communication issues, service problems, and a negative impact on your brand reputation.

Based on your long-term goals for growth and profitability, here is my conclusion on the two strategic options you face.

The decision to manage your warehouse internally or to outsource to a 3PL should be viewed as a choice between building an asset versus leveraging an asset.

For businesses with a long-term focus on growth and profitability, the most strategic choice is often to outsource to a 3PL.

Why Outsourcing is the Strategic Choice

1. Enables Focus on Core Business: Your company's long-term growth and profitability will be driven by your core competencies, sales, marketing, product development, and customer relationships. Outsourcing logistics allows you to dedicate your time, capital, and mental energy to these areas, which typically have a higher return on investment than managing warehouse operations.
2. Scalability and Flexibility: A 3PL provides immediate scalability. As your business grows, a 3PL can easily handle increased order volumes, seasonal spikes, and new market entries without requiring you to make significant, long-term capital investments in a new warehouse or technology. This flexibility is crucial for sustaining growth without straining your financial resources.
3. Risk Mitigation: A 3PL assumes the operational risks associated with warehousing, such as labor management, regulatory compliance, and a large portion of the capital investment in technology and infrastructure. By transferring this risk, you protect your business from potential financial

losses and distractions, allowing you to focus on strategic growth.

While the internal model (DIY) offers a high degree of control, it is often a path that demands too much of a growing company's resources, diverting them from the very activities that are essential for long-term growth and profitability. Outsourcing, when done with a carefully selected partner, is the most effective way to optimize logistics, reduce operational risk, and empower your business to focus on what truly matters for sustained success.